The Griffin Poetry Prize Anthology

The Griffin Poetry Prize Anthology

A selection of the 2006 shortlist

Edited by Lisa Robertson

ANANSI

Published in 2006 by
House of Anansi Press Inc.
110 Spadina Avenue, Suite 801
Toronto, ON, M5V 2K4
Tel. 416-363-4343
Fax 416-363-1017
www.anansi.ca

Distributed in Canada by
HarperCollins Canada Ltd.
1995 Markham Road
Scarborough, ON, M1B 4M8
Toll free tel. 1-800-387-0117

Distributed in the United States by
Publishers Group West
1700 Fourth Street
Berkeley, CA 94710
Toll free tel. 1-800-788-3123

The Griffin Trust and "POETRY" logos used with permission.
Page 95 constitutes a continuation of this copyright page.

10 09 08 07 06   1 2 3 4 5

LIBRARY AND ARCHIVES CANADA CATALOGUING IN PUBLICATION DATA

The Griffin poetry prize anthology : a selection of the
2006 shortlist / edited by Lisa Robertson.

ISBN 0-88784-742-0

1. English poetry — 21st century. 2. Canadian poetry (English) — 21st century.
I. Robertson, Lisa, 1961–

PS8293.1.G74 2006   821'.9208   C2005-907432-9

Library of Congress Control Number: 2006920153

Cover design: Scott Thornley & Co.
Cover photograph: Shin Sugino
Typesetting: Brian Panhuyzen

 Canada Council **Conseil des Arts**
for the Arts **du Canada**

ONTARIO ARTS COUNCIL
CONSEIL DES ARTS DE L'ONTARIO

*We acknowledge for their financial support of our publishing program
the Canada Council for the Arts, the Ontario Arts Council, and the Government of Canada
through the Book Publishing Industry Development Program (BPIDP).*

Printed and bound in Canada

CONTENTS

Elizabeth Winslow (translator)
Dunya Mikhail: *The War Works Hard*

Canadian Finalists

Phil Hall: *An Oak Hunch*

Sylvia Legris: *Nerve Squall*

Erín Moure: *Little Theatres*

PREFACE

Stacks of slippery slim volumes teetered on each surface in the house, open books skirted every comfortable chair, reading progressed even during meals and into the night, pages were turned down, spilled on, marked in pencil, notes accumulated, the occulist's prescription began to feel imprecise and the lamps were adjusted, last-minute shipments were signed for in haste, ad hoc shelving was devised, spouses and companions learned to expect limited conversation. Although in some ways it felt like a strange Wellesian aesthetic experiment in an acute form of reading, the honour of absorbing so many hundreds of books of poetry over just a couple of months was considerable: here was a rare chance to observe and assess this strange, loved art via a complete immersion in the syllables and ideas of a single year. Yet this intense readerliness was shot through with an inevitable anxiety. As Lavinia Greenlaw, Eliot Weinberger, and I read, we grimly noted the third year of the American and British war in Iraq. Cars burned and public buildings were looted all over France as the young people of impoverished suburban housing developments aggressively protested the deaths of Zyed Benna and Bouna Traore, who were electrocuted while hiding from police. Prisoners in Guantanamo Bay continued to be held illegally, against the protocols outlined by the Geneva Conventions, their very identities in a grey zone. Meanwhile, the U.S. Department of Homeland Security requires entrants' new passports to contain biometric identity chips. In France again, massive protests shut down sixty-three universities across the country as students refused the suspension of their rights to a socially equitable employment contract. On the way to meet with the other Griffin Prize judges on a March afternoon in Paris, I noted some of the graffiti at the embattled Sorbonne: *Nous n'aurons que ce que nous saurons prendre*; *Place de la Précarité*; *Destituer tous les Politiques*. I was reminded of the Roman Lucretius' urgent demand to Venus — to amorously sedate the lusty god of war long enough for the poem to be written, and then to be read.

The decisions we made together that afternoon were surprisingly simple and agreeable to reach — and I say surprisingly not just because there were many more very strong books meriting repeated reading and discussion, but because the three of us inevitably brought to our meeting very diverse political and cultural experiences, very different backgrounds as readers of poetry. Certainly the fact of speaking English seemed to us a cosmetic commonality. These seven books, then, whose many Englishes are thoroughly folded through with Arabic, Galician, East German, French, Carribean, the stuttering of the body, and the language of birds, answered our desires for poetry whose commitment to complexity greeted the multiple complexities of readers. Shot through with the tensions of multilingual musics, the erosion of liberatory notions of identity, post-colonial thinking, exile, and war, these poets are willing to head right into the crisis, the destitution, in political being. They insist on the necessity of the poem to engage fully in a description of the disturbance, even atrocity, of the present. Never placating, each presses towards the particularity of a form that can hold the many-voiced, the gorgeous chaos that moves us readers and writers to continue amidst impossibility.

Now, our living fraught and buckled by new communication and warfare technologies, we may no longer have the luxury to recall emotion in tranquility. These poets sculpt a different means of poesis, making. Indeed, they present us with models of incalculably intimate risk, each kinetically specific to our worldly mess. Their shapely excellence will perhaps not give any pause to the gods or machines of war. But it will give us readers ways to turn towards language as a force that invents and receives and holds the extremely precious and precarious world. This is poetry for untranquil readers who love and argue and discern.

— Lisa Robertson
April 2006

International Finalists

Kamau Brathwaite

Born to Slow Horses

To read Kamau Brathwaite is to enter into an entire world of human histories and natural histories, beautiful landscapes and their destruction, children's street songs, high lyricism, court documents, personal letters, literary criticism, sacred rites, eroticism and violence, the dead and the undead, confession and reportage. An epic of one man (containing multitudes) in the African diaspora, Brathwaite's world even has its own orthography and typography, demanding total attention to the poem, forbidding casual glances. *Born to Slow Horses* is a major book from a major poet. Here political realities turn into musical complexities, voices overlap, history becomes mythology, spirits appear in photographs. And, in what may well be the first enduring poem on the disaster of 9/11, Manhattan becomes another island in the poet's personal archipelago, as the sounds of Coleman Hawkins transform into the words and witnesses and survivors. Throughout *Born to Slow Horses*, as in his earlier books, Brathwaite has invented a new linguistic music for subject matter that is all his own.

from HAWK

And so this foreday morning w/out light or choice
i cannot swim
the stone. i can't hold on to water. so i drown

i swallow left. i turn & fall-
ow into fear & blight. a night so deep it make you turn
& weep the line of spiders of yr future you see spinn-

ing here. their silver
voice of tears. their lid. less jewel eyes .
all thru this buffeting eternity i toss i burn

and when i rise leviathan from the deep . black shining from my skin
of seals. blask tooth. less pebbles mine the shore
haunted by dust & bromes . wrist. watches w/out tone or tides. communion

w/out broken
hands. x-
plosions of frustration. the trans-

substantiation of the sweat
of hate. the absent ruby lips
upon the wrinkle rim

of wine . i wake to tick
to tell you that in these loud waters of my land
there is no root no hope no cloud no dream no sail canoe or dang. le miracle .

good day cannot repay bad *night.* our teeth snarl snapp-
ing even at halp-
less angels' evenings' meetings' melting steel

in this new farmer garden of the earth's delights
this staggering stranger of injustices
come rumbelling down the wheel and grave-

yard of the wind. down the scythe narrow streets. clear
air for a moment . clear
innocence whe we are running. *so so so so so many.* the crowd flow-

ing over Brooklyn Bridge. *so so so many . i had not thought death
had undone so many* . melting away into what is now sighing . light
calp from the clear avenue forever

our souls sometimes far out ahead already of our surfaces
and our life looking back
salt. as in Bhuj. in Grenada. Guernica. Amritsar. Tajikistan

the sulphur-stricken cities of the plains of Aetna. Pelée. ab Napoli & Krakatoa
the young window-widow baby-mothers of the prostitutes .
looking back looking back as in Bosnia. the Sudan. Chernobyl

Oaxaca terremoto incomprehende. al'fata el Jenin. the Bhopal
babies sucking toxic milk. our growing heavy furry tongues
accustom to the *what-is-the-word-that-is-not-here-in-English* beyond *schadenfreude*
not at all like *fado* or *duende*

So what is the word
for this high rafter of suicide. the dove of the rope
choking the sweet cooing throat of the priests of success. the shock

of yr death in the fission of indebtedness
quagmire . darfour. waste. quick-silver into quick-
sand & chute. **My Brother**'s soft bowels of aids. the youth of the full taste of death

in the uncouth cooper of water .
what prophet my tongue
w/the tsunami loss of my Mother the Noun. the fail-

ure of falling angelicas' hope. alphabets stuff upside-down
in my mouth. bandaloo
babel. and the down-

fall of plaster upon all these voices & scores
dub rap hip-hop scouse. the lock-
chain(ed) markets of marrakesh

seething old sores
of no longer verbs
that can heal. of no longer baptisms

that will bawl out yr name from the top of disaster
adjectives already gone a-
way clattering. lounging in shame. the silence of rot

of the hot of unheavens. the dread kapot
ovens of the beast upon the thrashing floor of syphillis. flat
foot of fear . the unknown animal that is now yr sibyl sister at the door

the four
little bombard girls of Birmingham that ku
klux christian tabernacle night in Sodom & Herero

the corn
husk terror of Rwanda. the poor who live bom-
fim the stony guts & gashes of our or-

nate palaces. the roses widow now for. ever reach-
ing in frus. tration in her open-limmo fire-
crack. ing back. seat for her hero hero presidential husband's blown-

out confetti brains in Dallas
the curling Black Death mushroom gloam
of God in Nagasaki . what Pol Pot did

King Leopold's Great Pyramid. of Skulls inside the Belgian Congo
like judas come to chrissmas. like leopard come to lamb
even upon this dark un. even catastrophic ground where soon

the devastation saurus faces of the dead will dyaam us fron-
tom from their rat. tle sockets. the gentle liquid iris language of their prayers .
soft blades of cyandle eyes in psalms of pain & irie innocence .

of ruin photographs & childhood teddy bears' young lighted flickering hearts
against the black & shining iron railings' incense of the parks
all their birds

gone
leaves' spirits of green vegetation's ceremonies
gone

Rita Lasar Joseph O'Reilly Masuda wa Sultan. her 19 children
gone
the Ladder 16 Crew. *so many thousands*

gone
it look like nearly evva one who went to work up they that way
is gone

like the day you make me swallow the tail of my tongue in the villages
following the foot-
steps of my own self my own self. the distress

of my own rivers of this flesh
mek dem kno wi feel
my own ash my own alph mi own outcry

how yu mek me sing these strange mesongs
in mi own *mantecs* poem so far from music sex and saxophone
& nothing nothing nothing new

all wreck(ed) . all wrack(ed) . and
falling from the blue
Iran Iraq Columbus Ayiti & Colombo . Beirut Manhattan & Afghanistan

I was standin on the steps of City Hall . . .in all that dust

. . .

and I knew that Terry [her husband the Captain of Rescue 11] wd have been

. . .

on one of the highest floor(s) that he cd get to. . .in that building

. . .

for that's what his Company does. . . and when I saw the building come down
I knew that he had no chance

. . .

Sometimes I start to worry that he was afraid. . .but. . . knowing him
I think he was completely focussed on the job at hand. . .sometimes it makes me angry

[she gives here a little laugh of pain]

but I don't think that he

. . .

I think in the back of his mind. . . he was more concerned about where
I was? and the fact that I was far-enough-away. . .from the trouble?
But I don't think that he considered. . . his not-coming-home

. . .

and sometimes that makes me angry. . .s'almost as if he didn't choose me. . .?
But I can't fault him for that he was doin his job. . .That's who he was
and why I lloved him so much

So I can't blame him for that

. . .

His friend Jim told me that he saw Terry going in and Terry said to him
we may not be seeing each other again
and kissed him on the cheek. . .and ran. . .upstairs [into the North Tower]

9

When the building came down

. . .

I just felt a complete disconnection in my heart

. . .

It was just like everything was just ripped-out-of-my-chest

. . .

I thought that Terry just

. . .

incinerated

. . .

I was grabbing the dust. . .from the ground. . . thinking that he was
in the dust

Beth Petrone speaking in the HBO/TV Memorial Tribute to the Heroes of 9/11
(26 May 2002)
. . .for her own beautiful self . and for all the women of this poem's world in New York Rwanda Kingston Iraq Afghanistan. . .

I lost my husband . . .but I think that he did. . .the best that he cd

. . .

because I truly believe that when Jerry got to Heaven. . . he had so many chips in his favor that he
bargained for this child because he knew that that wd be the one thing that wd save me

. . .

And. . . so I think in that respect(s)

. . .

I got. . .I. . .I . . .I'm go(ing) to live. . . I still have a part of Jerry

. . .

that I'm going to see in May. And a lot of apple people didn't get that

. . .

So I think that in certain ways. . .I was lucky   . But in other ways

[and here she tries to smile]

. . .obviously. . .I was not. . .
[and makes a wordless Sorry]

>

so let us even at this time

remember the poor & the helpless the cold the hungry
les damnés de la terre

the sick in mind & body . them that will bear
the broken fence of mourning on their faces
the lame the lonely the unnamed unloving the unloved

the jaded agèd in the name of God . the little trace. less concertina children grain-
ering the wheatless streets of Rio Mysore Srebrenitza
none who will now nor know the living loving-kindness of the Lord
upon another shore

And the tune almost gone now from the solo
just its soft shimmering skein of archipelagoes
just walter johnson & the boys holding you up in this

pool & spot. light's shapely union
of yr pyramid . the fallow folded metal leaves un
-folding to the slow. down-spiralling bell & tenor

of yr song

& fallin here like sparrowes feathers sorrowes
o my love
but tall still tall from where you have been cast. cast

down the walls of pomp & pride & vivid firnament
the wealthy many-eyed & pixie prison-homes
come rolling down the rumble

of the tide of thorn & rock. et refuse. thrones
thrones thrown down a Babylon where you a-
bide. defile. so many lynching afternoons ago

strange etching fruit of lonely crucifixions' systemat-
ically broken hands & broken catatonic bones. so
many broken guitar strings. such kernel damage

in the white-tile bathroom precincts. the mush
gomorrah broom-
stick up. o curling Hawk. yr spoken haitian anguish

                                                                    •
                                              w/yr frail fierce solo
                          burning in the changeling light w/in this room so blue
                                                        so indigo

                                          •

          the feathers fall. ing fly. ing fall. ing fail. ing fall
                          ing in this new
              new york monument of dying cold & aberfan

                      where so much glory has been pitch
                              & toss . green
          sun so bright the shadows when you walk in them

                  are red & burn. ing thorn & muharram
                  . so many many children abikú & born
          w/death. and their torn stories lost and nvr told

                                          •

Michael Hofmann (translator)

Durs Grünbein: *Ashes for Breakfast*

Born in Dresden, a "deathtrap / for angels," Durs Grünbein is the most significant poet to have emerged from the old East. His poems have a remarkable quality of contemplation, which enables them to shrug off pathos and irony, and so to reveal their personal and political depths. Unromantic, contained, but always moving and moved, he is ever alert to history's "sudden nearness" and brings it to us as mirror, window, and trapdoor. Michael Hofmann's translations are live-action engagements of one poet with another — of languages reacting, competing, consoling, and teasing — and propose new answers to old questions about whether poetry can travel this well or at all.

PORTRAIT OF THE ARTIST AS A YOUNG BORDER DOG (NOT COLLIE)

To the memory of I. P. Pavlov
And all the laboratory dogs
Of the medical academy of the
Russian armed forces

Frozen dog
Brought back to life.

"Astonishing!" called the man
With the reedy voice.

"And he's not the only one,"
replied the stranger.

(to be continued)

1

Being a dog is an empty car park at noon.
"Nothing but trouble . . ." and seasickness on land.
Being a dog is this and that, taking instruction from garbage heaps,
A knuckle sandwich for dinner, mud orgasms.
Being a dog is whatever happens next, randomness
The mother of boredom and incomprehension.
Being a dog is being up against a bigger opponent
Time, which does you in with endless chain-links.
So much of too-much in a tiny space . . .
Being a dog is a ride on the ghost train of language,
Which keeps throwing clever obstructions your way.
Being a dog is having to when you don't want to, wanting to
When you can't, and always somebody watching.
Being a dog?
              It's the bad smell attaching to your words.

2

"Get out of the light," you say, talking to the demon
In the glass gone blind with looking,
Giving you the glad eye these many years.
Its harsh glance pierces your face
Like a spy from the clan of the X-ray spirits.
When you turn your back, your fear of
Going rigid turns with you.
Till something's certain . . .
                              behind the grins.
Even in your phantom image, the brain scan
Picks you out. If only partially.
An alien among aliens, you stand out
As they stand out in you.
                      With walled up frontal bone
Every refuge is left behind you. Will it be too late
By the time the autopsy sheds its bit of light?

3

... umpteen years of service with a view of barbed wire fence,
Trotting back and forth upcountry and down, only a dog could endure,
Captivated by his lead, trained to behave from infancy.
Even asleep, the tiny gap in the wire
Shrinks to the size of a bullet hole behind his ear.
A smacking of the lips proves even dogs have dreams.
The thing that sets his juices flowing is the idea
That parallel lines meet somewhere.
Where Pavlov stands for the residue of spirit
(instinct mobilized, a zigzag compass)
Dialectics is nothing but ... dumb loyalty;
An ear for the feeling in his master's voice.
The moment of clarity is the lightening before death,
At the end of the trial.
                    "Like a dog."

4

You look old, young hound. Atom age old.
Curious in the mornings, heavy with leftover scraps
Of vivid dreams, you amble into your day,
Penned in by the traffic streaming by, the lingo
Printed on flattened wood pulp, the mush
It takes plenty of cunning not to gag on.
Because what you are supposed to be, your phenotype
The fetish, broadcasts to everyone: a German.
White . . . male . . . medium build . . . brown hair.
                                        It might do
For seventy years of existential struggle.
At best, patience might hold back the drool.
But the greatest threat, even to you,
Is from stupidity,
                    the buzz of brain activity,
Of which it's said, it creates itself.

5

From the junked buzz of the early years,
Led out on to the black ice of shy objectivity,
You go rigid at zero with an excess of signifiers.
The roar of empty promises,
Vacuuming out words, gestures, expressions.
The garish dreams lighten in the laundry,
Chemically bleached, printed with some nonsense or other.
Resistance at the century's end retreats
Blatantly into the brain.
The only thing to keep you up, simpleton, is laughter
At an animal caught in its own toils.
It's the only thing you could begin to take seriously.
Asked what I've spent night and day thinking about,
I sometimes have the presence of mind to reply: "Nothing."

6

Homo sap., the animal with letters after its name,
The only one to lie, to obey the logic
Of appearance and deception. As you'll see
If you cast your eye once over a newspaper.
Twice . . . careful now . . . and you're caught.
What good is your skepticism when so much is taken on trust.
When you breathe (like nitrogen) illusions
That are rumored to be the stuff of dreams.
Bit player, with your head in the fog,
Think of Socrates.
                    When he swore, "By my dog!"
A world of opinions smashed to smithereens.
As any child will tell you, the very first word
Paradoxically produces a misunderstanding
That it takes repetition to clear.

7

I was happy in a sandy no-man's-land, I didn't do verbals,
I was a dog, wanting for nothing or not much.
The faith I needed to live by came down from on high.
God was an airplane, camouflaged like a cloud
By the enemy, remote-controlled, to lull me to sleep.
But I remained stoical, eyeing my terrain.
When I stood to attention on all fours,
With my dynamited pelt, the ground earthed me.
In the West, so they said, the dog precedes
His master.
               In the East, he trails him — at a distance.
As for me, I was my own dog,
In the suicide strip, equidistant from East and West.
It was only here that I sometimes performed
My *salto mortale* in the gloaming between dog and wolf.

8

Reason, as Joe says, this two-bit hell
Is this place where the self whistles up a storm;
Where fear and curiosity strike a balance.
Fear: lest it suddenly disappear
Without trace on the path of curiosity.
Curiosity: what it might be like, to live without fear.
It produces a little drama
Along the border marked by reason
Through perpetually new straying.
I am not here, it says.
                              I am not there.
And its games of hide and go seek confirm:
I is none other than this border dog
Keeping a watchful eye on itself.
Who will guarantee that it won't leap on you
If you quietly remove yourself from circulation?

9

Now listen to this: in the obituary they wrote about me
In my lifetime, they said I was so sweet-natured
That they wanted to keep me as a pet.
It makes me ill to hear them drooling
About my loyalty, my affection, my trustworthiness around children.
Tripe! There's a term for everything alien.
Looks as though time has caught up with me,
And my voice is swimming in the confession:
"I was half zombie, half *enfant perdu* . . ."
Perhaps eventually space gulped me down
Where the horizon closes up.
My double can look after me from here on in.
My orneriness is puked out, plus the question:
Do pets have lighter brains?

10

Just as well you can't read my thoughts,
The film I've got running in my imagination.
"My life in reverse . . ." or how I blindly
Patrolled the minefields in no-man's-land,
Myself just a cipher in a simultaneous equation.
No longer simultaneous, and I'm free.
The landscape sinks back, a new brownfield site.
Ever since I got out of here, no one knows me anymore.
The sand blots.
                    Guard towers are forgetful
As eyes, relieved by sockets.
The two or three names for the place of separation
Are already gone.
                        Now nothing is left to recall the trick
By which a strip of land became a hole in time.
Just as well you can't read my thoughts.

11

And you? Have you forgotten where you're from?
Is it starting to dawn on you how much damage was done
By so many years of humiliation and slapstick?
What a country, where a word on something topical
Provokes more than the unsayable
Remaining unsaid!
                              Whose voice
Is swallowed during the attempt to chew your gubbins?
To cotton on right away to what's happening, and what isn't
Can be sophistication.
                              In this instance, it was lethargy
That prompted you to stand to attention brain-dead with exhaustion.
What is life anyway? Everything's replaceable
Where hypnosis rules and *my duty right or wrong*.
Don't kid yourself, in the paradise of dogs
Piss on a tree trunk is the stuff of dreams.

Dog among dogs awake at night in the firing zone:
    How was it again, your stomach growled? What at?
    At the biscuits they tossed you in Prussia?
What was it that kicked you in the back,
Was it the cerebral cortex that said, "I know"?
    Was it the supply of fresh blood?
What a dog's life, and at what a price.
    No underdog-victim twaddle, please.

It takes ethnographers, with their coconspirators' look,
    To understand fear. Animals often appear as humans
    In their works. As far as I'm concerned,
I was embarked on a long sleep. I was a machine
That liked it when my buttons were pushed.
    So and so many strikes per minute. I struck. They struck.
For the apprehensive, the quickest way from A to B
    (and back again) is the ellipse.

Break a leg . . . Artificial intelligence
    Has planned ahead in the event of a breakdown.
    The only question remaining is
Who will fix you if your machinery breaks.
As an *homme machine*, you enjoy La Mettrie's
    Protection, and don't need an alibi.
You function, that's enough.
    And good old Hobbes will pay the bill.

Unless he's tried shock treatment, no one can say
    What he lacks. Plunged from ignorance,
    Your whole life opens up. In free fall,
A projector scans the table of defeats.
Punched strips of naked fear. Things go black
    Before your eyes. Could be dazzlement
That says it wasn't Vico or Machiavelli
    Who said history is blind in both eyes.

Michael Palmer

Company of Moths

"How listen, where dwell?" asks Michael Palmer in a book whose continuous questioning only ever opens out to the surprising generosity of a kind of equivocation. That is, more questions, rather than a rectitude, follow from reflection, and they are the kinds of familiar questions we pose to a companion we love: "What of that wolfhound at full stride?"; "Did the glare bother us?"; "Can you hear what I'm thinking, . . . ?" His sequences shimmer on the edge of the surreal, scattering the suggestions of a symbolic plenitude that pertains to a life lived with a dexterous consciousness of the necessity of transience. This is the world in its multiple thing-ness, with no gratuitous attitudinizing.

"The rats outnumber the roses in our garden. That's why we've named it The Rat Garden."

A discussion of the sublime ensued. Aunt Klara served her ginger-peach tea. At ninety-six, many of her parts still worked. "It is life that should inspire fear, not death," she would say, quoting the Dietrich once again.

It was the first May Day of the new millennium, though no one could recall what that day meant. "Perhaps it is the day when the rat lies down with the rose," tiny Perdita remarked. All were aghast, as these were the first words she had ever uttered.

The skywriters were active that near windless day, their most frequent message, in cursive, "Rats Rule!" Slowly the letters would thicken and belly out toward the east, then dissolve into illegible smoke.

The sun declined; the mayflies made their entrance, and the sedulous bats.

Then the great evening feast was placed before us: pea soup with pork knuckle; the little *elver*, baby eels, almost transparent, quickly boiled and served with mashed turnip; and of course the goose, stuffed with Nuremberg sausage, chestnuts, onion, chopped carrot and cream; and finally a Black Forest cake, that baroque confection of chocolate, whipped cream, sweetened cherries and kirsch.

It was over coffee and brandy, as the evening drew to a close, that Uncle Johann suddenly blurted out, "I'm sorry, I know I'm a terrible poet." At that moment Perdita formed the second sentence of her inchoate life, "All poets know they are terrible."

THE

The red vowels, how they spill
then spell a sea of red

And the bright ships —
are they not ghost ships

And the bridge's threads
against flame-scarred hills

And us outside
by other worlds

SO

So the promise of happiness?
he asked a frog

then swallowed the frog
And the buzz of memory?

he asked the page
before lighting the page

And by night the sliding stars
beyond the night itself

A

A table erased
It is not realism makes possible the feast

Grey face turned away
Jam jar of forget-me-nots

Girl with gold chain
cinching her waist

But is it true
And what will become of us

AS

As if the small voices —
one-erum two-erum

pompalorum jig
wire briar broken lock

then into and into
the old crow's nest —

and so when young,
before all the rest

CREASE

Crease in the snowy field
of evening within us

How the owl stares
and startles there

fashioning mindless elegy
So the remembered world's

songs and flooded paths
This heap of photographs

THIS

This perfect half-moon
of lies in the capital

Crooks and fools in power what's new
and our search has begun for signs of spring

Maybe those two bluebirds
flashing past the hawthorn yesterday

Against that, the jangle of a spoon in a cup
and a child this day swept out to sea

BUT

But the birth and death of stars?
The birds without wings,

wings without bodies?
The twin suns above the harbor?

The accelerating particles?
The pools of spilled ink?

Pages turning themselves
in The Paper House?

SOON

Soon the present will arrive
at the end of its long voyage

from the Future-Past to Now
weary of the endless nights in cheap motels

in distant nebulae
Will the usual host

of politicians and celebrities
show up for the occasion

or will they huddle out of sight
in confusion and fear

DREAM OF A LANGUAGE THAT SPEAKS

Hello Gozo, here we are,
    the spinning world, has

it come this far?
    Hammering things, speeching them,

nailing the anthrax
    to its copper plate,

matching the object to its name,
    the star to its chart.

(The sirens, the howling machines,
    are part of the music it seems

just now, and helices of smoke
    engulf the astonished eye;

and then our keening selves, Gozo,
    whirled between voice and echo.)

So few and so many,
    have we come this far?

Sluicing ink onto snow?
    I'm tired, Gozo,

tired of the us/not us,
    of the factories of blood,

tired of the multiplying suns
    and tired of colliding with

the words as they appear
    without so much as a "by your leave,"

without so much as a greeting.
    The more suns the more dark —

is it not always so —
    and in the gathering dark

Ghostly Tall and Ghostly Small
    making their small talk

as they pause and they walk
    on a path of stones,

as they walk and walk,
    skeining their tales,

testing the dust,
    higher up they walk —

there's a city below,
    pinpoints of light —

high up they walk,
    flicking dianthus, mountain berries,

turk's-caps with their sticks.
    Can you hear me? asks Tall.

Do you hear me? asks Small.
    Question pursuing question.

And they set out their lamp
    amid the stones.

for Yoshimasu Gozo

Elizabeth Winslow (translator)

Dunya Mikhail: *The War Works Hard*

We know that Dunya Mikhail was raised in Saddam's Iraq and sent into exile to follow the news of its devastation from afar. So the very first line of *The War Works Hard* comes as a surprise: "What good luck!" The second line crystallizes both the contemporary reality and Mikhail's sensibility: "She has found his bones." In her poems, war is a monstrous fact of ordinary life, and her particular skill is the invention of unadorned images that capture the often unexpected human responses. Brecht wrote, "We'd all be human if we could," and Mikhail, despite all the contrary evidence, shows that we can, and sometimes are. These are political poems without political rhetoric, Arabic poems without Arabic poetical flourishes, an exile's letter with neither nostalgia nor self-pity, an excavation of the ruins of her homeland where the Sumerian goddess Inanna is followed on the next page by the little American devil Lynndie England. In Elizabeth Winslow's perfect translations, poetry takes on its ancient function of restoring meaning to the language. Here is the war in Iraq in English without a single lie.

AMERICA

Please don't ask me, America.
I don't remember
on which street,
with whom,
or under which star.
Don't ask me . . .
I don't remember
the colors of the people
or their signatures.
I don't remember if they had
our faces
and our dreams,
if they were singing
or not,
writing from the left
or the right
or not writing at all,
sleeping in houses
on sidewalks
or in airports,
making love or not making love.
Please don't ask me, America.
I don't remember their names
or their birthplaces.
People are grass —
they grow everywhere, America.
Don't ask me . . .
I don't remember
what time it was,
what the weather was like,
which language,
or which flag.
Don't ask me . . .

I don't remember
how long they walked under the sun
or how many died.
I don't remember
the shapes of the boats
or the number of stops . . .
How many suitcases they carried
or left behind,
if they came complaining
or without complaint.
Stop your questioning, America,
and offer your hand
to the tired
on the other shore.
Offer it without questions
or waiting lists.
What good is it to gain the whole world
if you lose your soul, America?
Who said that the sky
would lose all of its stars
if night passed without answers?
America, leave your questionnaires to the river
and leave me to my lover.
It has been a long time,
we are two distant, rippling shores
and the river wriggles between us
like a well-cooked fish.
It has been a long time, America,
(longer than the stories of my grandmother
in the evening)
and we are waiting for the signal
to throw our shell in the river.
We know that the river is full

of shells
this last one
wouldn't matter,
yet it matters to the shell . . .
Why do you ask all these questions?
You want our fingerprints
in all languages
and I have become old,
older than my father.
He used to tell me in the evenings
when no trains ran:
One day, we will go to America.
One day, we will go
and sing a song,
translated or not translated,
at the Statue of Liberty.
And now, America, now
I come to you without my father.
The dead ripen faster
than Indian figs,
but they never grow older, America.
They come in shifts of shadow and light
in our dreams
and as shooting stars
or curve in rainbows
over the houses we left behind.
They sometimes get angry
if we keep them waiting long . . .
What time is it now?
I am afraid I will receive
your registered mail, America,
in this hour
which is good for nothing . . .

So I will toy with the freedom
like teasing a pet cat.
I wouldn't know what else
to do with it
in this hour
which is good for nothing . . .
And my sweetheart
there, on the opposite
shore of the river
carries a flower for me.
And I — as you know —
dislike faded flowers.
I do like my sweetheart's handwriting
shining each day in the mail.
I salvage it from among ad fliers
and a special offer:
"Buy One Get One Free"
and an urgent promotional announcement:
"Win a million dollars
if you subscribe to this magazine!"
and bills to be paid
in monthly installments.
I like my sweetheart's handwriting,
though it gets shakier every day.
We have a single picture
just one picture, America.
I want it.
I want that moment
(forever out of reach)
in the picture which I know
from every angle:
the circular moment of sky.
Imagine, America,

if one of us drops out of the picture
and leaves the album full
of loneliness,
or if life becomes
a camera
without film.
Imagine, America!
Without a frame,
the night will take us
tomorrow,
darling,
tomorrow
the night
will take us
without a frame.
We will shake the museums
forever from their sleep,
fix our broken clocks
so we'll tick in the public squares
whenever the train
passes us by.
Tomorrow,
darling,
tomorrow
we will bloom:
two leaves of a tree
we will try not to be
too graceful and green
and in time
we will tumble down like dancers
taken by the wind
to the places whose names
we'll have forgotten.

We will be glad for the sake of turtles
because they persist along their way . . .
Tomorrow
darling,
tomorrow,
I'll look at your eyes
to see your new wrinkles,
the lines of our future dreams.
As you braid my gray hair
under rain
or sun
or moon,
every hair will know
that nothing happens
twice,
every kiss a country
with a history
a geography
and a language
with joy and sadness
with war
and ruins
and holidays
and ticking clocks . . .
And when the pain in your neck returns, darling,
you will not have time to complain
and won't be concerned.
The pain will remain inside us
coy as snow that won't melt.
Tomorrow, darling,
tomorrow,
two rings will jingle
in the wooden box.

They have been shining for a long time
on two trembling hands,
entangled
by the absence.
Tomorrow,
the whiteness will expose
all its colors
as we celebrate the return
of what was lost
or concealed
in the whiteness.
How should I know, America,
which of the colors
was the most joyful
tumultuous
alienated
or assimilated
of them all?
How would I know, America?

THE RESONANCE

The resonance inside me
finally fell into the water.
On the shore of the world I sit looking at it,
and you watch me from the other shore.
You watch the sound as it fades away.
You watch the ripples as they disappear.
You watch the stars swing down.
You watch silver gleam on the scales of fish.
You watch something that breaks under the sun.
You watch as I dive into the sound,
and then you reach out

ح ب ال/ص و ت ك / أ ل ش م س ي / ف ن ا ل ه ا / أ ل
ر ن ي ن

Hibal sutek il-shamsy fanalaha-il-raneen:
Ropes of your sun-filled sound are reined by the resonance.
The letters spread in the water like this:

ح ب / ا ل ص و ت / ك ا ل ش م س / ي ف ن ا / ل ه ـ / أ
ل ر ن ي ن

Hub il-sut kal-shamsi yafna lahu il-raneen:
Love of the sound is like the sun
for which the resonance will perish.

The hypothesis: I am tense and so are you.
We neither meet nor separate.

The desired result: We meet in the absence.

The proof: As tension turns people into arcs, we are two arcs.
We neither meet nor separate (the hypothesis)
so we must be parallel.
If two parallel lines are bisected by a third line
(in this case, the line of tension)
their corresponding angles must be equal (a geometrical theorem).
So we are congruent (because shapes are congruent
when their angles are equal)
and we form a circle (since the sum
of two congruent arcs
is a circle).
Therefore, we meet in the absence
(since the circumference of a circle
is the sum of contiguous points
which can each be considered
a point of contact).

NOTHING HERE IS ENOUGH

I need a parrot,
identical days,
a quantity of needles,
and artificial ink
to make history.

I need veiled eyelids,
black lines,
and ruined puppets
to make geography.

I need a sky wider than longing,
and water that is not H_2O
to make wings.

The days are no longer enough
to distinguish the missing.
I no longer see you
because I no longer dream.
I offer a tear to the rain
as if scattering you
in the Dead Sea,
and in order to sing you,
I need glass to muffle the sound.

WHAT'S NEW?

I saw a ghost pass in the mirror.
Someone whispered something in my ear.
I said a word, and left.
Graves were scattered with mandrake seeds.
A bleating sound entered the assembly.
Gardens remained hanging.
Straw was scattered with the words.
No fruit is left.
Someone climbed on the shoulders of another.
Someone descended into the netherworld.
Other things are happening
in secret.
I don't know what they are —
this is everything.

Canadian Finalists

Phil Hall

An Oak Hunch

These are poems of ferocity and humility, of vulnerability and wit, poems whose skilled complexities elucidate the lyric disturbance of melody, memory, and self. Grasping his intimate line like a kind of loved and fortuitous hand tool, what Phil Hall constructs is a voice that attends to the familial and psychic histories submerged in landscape, in all their bitterness and gorgeousness. There is a rough amplitude in his compositional principle: that "between the body & language / a ravine of call & response." In this work, out of the uncertainty and lag of dailiness comes the knowledge that although precision isn't always simple, by the precise ear we may arrive at the heart.

from GANK PLUCK

THESE PRESBYTERIAN HIGHLANDS SNIFFED
indignant to be demonized by tiny limestone bones

the pouting shadow of a fresh hole might blaspheme
twist a perfectly graceful egg-gathering hand

to a gnarled gizzard only good for hanging a toy purse on
each Sunday — a tissue back of a clasp

I saw Byron Lambert in the school furnace room
take off his overalls & put on a beard over his beard

I grant each year its glowing paunch & shank
not mummery — each stark as the first years I knew here

the Salvation Army's bushel of puzzles & molded hair
its turkey pond-hard (the blind horse's eye) — some doing

to tenderize it all now as game — gobble — gravy — wish
get away from me with that CBC pander-mulch frippery

the fossils in the stone piles are talking to me their chalk

I CAN HEAR MY HEART — THE CLOCK — MY BREATH
imagine pronouns metamorphosing to sea beasts

saidiment running & flapping & lifting silt — my heart's
becoming Shelley's horse — the clock's becoming Byron's

my breath almost the tide's askew crochet
little words & big Romantics gallop through me together

as in *Julian and Maddalo* — the heart or the clock is throwing a shoe
the vellum-bloused gods love to bugger up the rhythm & the key

one *here*'s stuck in a glint-pull of backwash ago

OUR LITTLE CIVIC IS TOTALLED LOVE
& coming toward us out of the fog
  is the uncoupled next train of everyone
southbound to the U.S. tonight

we can run into the cornfield
the so many stones of us lunging
  the so many hands of us clear
popping the sockets of the dry stalks

  until it seems the fog has bones
that are pioneer documents
  being shredded & then absorbed
into the fog we are gulping

  as we turn to listen to the lengthened roar
think of all the times over the years
  we have noticed our own reflections in windows
& looked away or through ourselves

  at *what is really there*
a stack of transparencies
  the stills of an animated short
two cadavers named Adam & Eve

our first & last selves — frozen
we dyed their insides orange & blue
  thinly sliced them crown to heel
& photographed each slice

  sped up in sequence
the body comes at us like art
  as we hurtle through
listen to them all back there

crying to be prized free
from the blown rust dahlias
of the tail lights in the fog & the high beams
screening wide against cotton-batting

soon we will hear the local sirens
& scream to be casualties among them

THE MARBLE BARGE ONE EMPRESS BUILT — WELL
had built for Her Unearthliness — surprise — sank

Mao dredged its imperial decadence up — well
his officials had it dredged up — deslimed by regiments

& set on pylons in the Summer Palace lagoon
where Yankee Dog tourists & lowly Bethune-kin

walk on it — & it seems to float . . .

I will always — well — awhile — be grateful
to the goddess of inequality — *Seems-To*

that geranium-rose resorting to rouge & gin
mother gone bad — uneaten — powdery with mould

her gank pluck keeps killing itself
in a rented room not found till the smell

the concierge & the constable pounding . . .

hewn — rock-hedged — crofts stacked
cog-dumb up Irish sea crags know her — as do

hutongs (the narrow alleys of China) — bicycle
tube roofs & broken-brick soup steaming — she is

the grin of the stuffed fox in the glass box
& the grimace of goat carcass roped in seaweed . . .

the ark of necessity's pelted hard yet
which is why we still need to be twos

keep dry & fed a dog a cat a budgie
in open doorway ramparts lean — gawk

patchwork-eyed over & out at the deluge
name it *Seems-To* — claim it *treasure*

PAINTING THE SAW — I TRY TO PUT IT TO EARNED REST
it smears — guffaws — moans eerie — snags lace

all I've seen deserves a handle & teeth
slowly the hollow becomes the *holler* & files become *flies*

each fresh dab is a landing light for prodigal errors
the red mailbox flag is up & the stiff chimney smoke twines

Thomas Hart Benton — El Greco — & I
barking at a knot in barbershop harmony

while Frankie & Johnny — St. Augustine — & Dad
lean in under a hood — conferring

each body drawn a long wrong way that hurts loud
our lanky muscles destined for the luthier / mill

AT DUSK I WOULD STOP WRITING a prayer to things
handled badly, and lifting the usual cup, snorkel
into St. James Necropolis.

FROM PLOSIVE TO DIGRAPH, from willseed to
peregrination, over the peaks of the resolute hills,
through the windows of the tall buildings, I was
alphabetizing the obvious (a chickadee — a minted
toothpick — a crying-at-bingo smell).

Saying the old, chipped words, I liked to think
I was helping *them* pray too — *words don't know
how to read, books don't know how to read — they need
my weak eyes* — I thought, like some missionary to
island lepers — but I was the one banished to an
island — and the words were the missionaries —
I am the one with these stinking wounds in the
palms of my hands — these gifts? — my articulate
hands that can not make straight arrows.

*Pity Philoctetes, ye summer boaters, who roar past his
island in your floppy hats, flinging empty beer cans at
his pines — the epauletteless shadow of the blackbird
flies out of your marshes too — its flight a red and
yellow wound, its cry a coffin hinge.*

BECAUSE OF WHAT HAD HAPPENED to me at five, a
chainsaw was talking for the trees, a witness nerve in
the brain had crimped, my bed had lost its motor and
anchor, paragraphs blurred — beneath this weak chin,
all night surf barter, bawl.

Then a white shirt would open a stone foundation, a
man would walk through half of the sun, a preacher's
motorless car would be attacked by a "rainsaw".

Don't spare me the details — I blustered — *blood fills the
peninsulas — bottom is ribbed.*

LONG BEFORE MY OWN HUNGER (for what I used not
to know), The Great Hunger had destroyed crop after
crop of my ancestors — their thin muscles looking up
through my skin like eels through ice, their dead skin
running out onto the docks of my hair, desperate for
passage — I had to eat their stories to know them, had
to plant and plow under their little songs in mine.

*While I tore eczema scabs raw in sleep, or coughed up
chunks of brown phlegm, Meatboy, whom no one saw, saw
me, his mask — intrinsic as marrow to gesture, the dry bone
fit over the eye, cousin, abuser.*

Confusing brightness with health, adventure with
trauma, torn between the self-sufficiency of epigram
and tragedy's cast of millions, I held my title pages
up to the light — saw ricocheting hairy words of hoof-
white feather flame — saw *The Great Escape* eighteen
times, *The Field* almost as often.

I'D LOST MY LAP, WAS ROAMING THE STREETS, a mess and a failure, too old, no longer believing — but I had been taught mockingbirds well, kept waking up dreaming of gods and Wagner.

Asleep in a rented tuxedo, I'd be standing in the dark doorway of a barn, listening to little outboard waves crawl up a shore — *the lake's transparent toenails* I'd mumble, pleased with myself.

"Each one of us is two stupid birds," said Killdeer (who is also Owl) when he heard that howler about the lake's toenails.

AT 14, ALL I WANTED WAS TO SEE a girl naked — then my mother died, hers an open coffin, too naked for me — now I walk on the thread of my daughter's safety, my mother's features buried and strewn — one of the names I come to: "Populi".

Originally, the 22 shell I dropped into my father's coffin was a patricide-sinker to keep him below — but it has hollowed and lightened with time, become a tiny thermos of tears, the little I can give to quench his routes.

Open my face like a tackle box on a floor beside a crib again — can't we forget this alone business — can we still recite from memory Oppen's complete *Of Being Numerous* — "the shipwreck / of the singular" — though our shared dreams have turned to faded orange?

READING MYSELF (PLANKTON) reading other men
(schools) — Neruda's hunger a kindling, Mandelstam's
candle impatiently idling (*come on, get in*), Rupert Brooke's
nude statue on Skyros a site from which to hurl my ashes
at the same Elytis blue I always wanted to paint my rented
walls.

To explain what we have done with our bodies, Serenity
comes a day late with an entourage of boistrosities, like
always — silica, the current, the stone vote translated, the
two most important words in meat, *"The Charge of the
Greys"* and greens.

Trees creaking in the wind (like doors — and me leaking
prayer), patio chairs stacked in water, our cages waiting on
rubber wheels — this has nothing to do with you, the
Absolutely Sure — nothing to do with your old purple
vinegar myth.

WHEN WE ARE SCREAMING AT EACH OTHER AGAIN,
remember the time we tried to kill hate and eat it, or the
time we tried to live above beauty on the shores of the
burrow's vision — like flies — *Y Yo Y Yo Y Yo Y Yo Y Yo* . . .

Cemetery swimmer at dawn, wrung out and shaken,
wallow-fecund — I wash our bowls and set them out
(butternut and blackthorn) — try to wave to selfyeast — hear
myself being called by a candle being blown out — *ph.*

Though we all sink back together into the masks in the
words, the anguish of balance has cost us each something
we swore we wouldn't give up for anything.

OR SOMETHING WE KNEW WE HAD TO GIVE UP if
we wanted to live — my back townships
acquiescing in the rain . . .

I hold the blunt end of the pen in my mouth,
and put my palms together so the stinking holes
in my hands make one hole I can see through.

Bowing my head, I shove the pen through the
hole in my hands — *planchette!*

SAYING A LOST PATH BACK, as of old . . .

Sylvia Legris

Nerve Squall

Sylvia Legris's high-octane poems are powered by "atmospheric overload." Her eye is that of the twenty-first century — zooming from satellite to microscope — but her focus and coherence are increasingly rare in this age. In her hands, language refracts in ways which break open etymology to bring us more sense rather than less. Legris's poems build like chords from sub- to super-sonic and, even at their most rapid and heightened point, sustain the force of poetic enquiry. There is always, as she says, "something on your hook, / you feel it."

STRANGE BIRDS; TWITCHING BIRDS

1

Holy Bone Pickers! Holy Bird Mutations! Terminal Highway just lingers and lingers — unpleasant aftertaste and *maddening* jingles in your head (*Double-your-pleasure? Double-your-pain?*). Nostrils stinging of hot rubber, Firestone-fast food . . . and now what? Roadkill phantoms? Circling above you heat mirages?

No
    such
        luck.

The pluck-ugliest birds you'll ever see. Lizard-naked skulls, red-raw skin (Homely monks! who marinate in the bath too long — brush scrub and flagellation . . . *Count-your-tormented-prayers, birds.*).

Opportunistic birds. Birds who strike while the flesh is still hot. Incessant pickers; nitpickers. (Wash your hands a thousand times and still

these vultures get under your skin.)

—

Pick-pick-pick-pick-pick. Crawling with buzzing things and microscopic buzzards, little beaks, little pecks. Unnerving paresthesia (epidermal pointillism): a continent's worth of peck-marks, your body a stormy rash of range-map and no relief in sight! Out-of-kilter flight paths; shaky-on-takeoff navigation. (*Migratosis neurosis?*)

OCD: Overshadowing Condor Distress. Fear of bald-headed birds.

2

O little gull, little gull (*Larus minutus*). O Bonaparte's gull. (*Hey! Keep those coverts where I can see them.*)

Little gull, Lilliputian gull. Consumed with small galling swimming birds, the tiniest things send you wet-browed and reeling (eddying out of control and the weir has never looked so good).

—

Kittiwake Kittiwake Kittiwake (*getaway-getaway-getaway*).

Thorny nerves and bird-suspended bridges. O *frigate frigate* frigatebirds — even pelicans won't look you in the eye. The sky creepy with rooks and here you are, condemned, to the wrong side of the boardwalk — *checkcheckcheckcheckcheck checkcheck* — a never-ending game you are destined to bungle.

3

Kitchen Hell. Recipe Doom.

Lose your way in eggshells and fowl drippings. Falling-from-grace Angel Cake. Burnt-to-a-crisp Devil's Food. Bad leavening. Blood-curdling milk. And birds HARASSING HARASSING HARASSING you from stove to fridge and back.

Echolalic birds . . . TEA-KETTLE TEA-KETTLE TEA-KETTLE . . . Mimicking birds . . . DRINK-YOUR-TEA-EE-EE-EE . . .

— *they've got their nerve!* Repetitious birds! Ornithological tautologies!

—

. . . CHECKCHECKCHECKCHECKCHECK

Piebird, ovenbird: Off. Off. Off. Check the stove again and again. Chicken grease on the element? (CHECK) Fear of fire? (CHECK) Fear of flame? (CHECK CHECK-CHECK)

What a witches' sabbath of wings
— Robinson Jeffers

4

Little bird, little bird, LET ME OUT. *Not-a-chance Not-a-chance Forget-get-get-get-it . . .*

Damn this cracked crow! Damn this wicked net! A snare of ritual and vexation: Icterinæ Tyranny. Grackle Sacrament. Sins of the Feather. Banging your head till you're blackbird and blue.

All the time in Hell on your hands and an eternity of bird devotions on an endless string of millet . . . Ave Aviary, Ave Oriole, Hail Bob-bob-bob Bobolink . . .

———

Dead of night and captive to an unremitting chorus of blackbirds: Rusty Falsetto (creaking demons and doors and coming unhinged!), Nasal-Toned Tricolour (triple-glazed windows, blue-in-the-face), *Quiscalus mexicanus* . . . Arriba! Arriba! Arriba!

Grisly dreams. A palpitating litany of shadowy birds: *Quiscalus quiscula* (Commonest Common Grackle), *Euphagus cyanocephalus* (Brewer's Blackbird, volcanic stomach), *Euphagus* . . . esophagus (a nagging bird in the throat and your hands

won't stop trembling).

5

Unshakable birds! (Being followed? Being watched?) Run run but never escape the flutter of wings in your chest.

—

Demon-faced birds stare daggers from building ledges and at every corner you turn (*every corner you turn!*) . . . Twitching birds (nit-crawling catastrophe carriers), Tourettic birds (*odious-odious-odious*), birds skulking in turrets (Stone-Feathered Gargoyles, your cries for help

just so much sputtering).

—

Featherless. *Hopeless!* Overwhelmed with bird urges and the compulsion to tic the compulsion to tic the compulsion . . .

Are you dreaming? Are you sleeping? (*Dormez-vous? Dormez-cheep-cheep . . .*)

AGITATED SKY ETIOLOGY

STUMPED SKY (QUESTIONS OF MISSING WEATHER AND BIRDS)

1

Typical typical typical. A recent affinity for birds and now where are they?
No wings, no leaves. Just nerves crunching underfoot.

Wrong season for pelicans and geese and now a gaggle of goosebumps
erupting omens and Braille up your skin. You are ill at ease

with interpretation. (Reading the snow for signs
does nothing to take the chill off.) Overhead,
ice-capped birds shriek *Defeat! Defeat!*

2

Lack-Lack-Lack. Lonely ducks plead for rain but rain rain's gone away and the trees
have pulled inside themselves (multi-stumped and trunks
a frazzle of missing leaves).

Weather is numb. Nonsensical. The sky all thumbs and fingers falling.
What's the point here, what's the point there: unceasing questions.

Clouds a flummox of fluster. Flux. Ice miasma. (Second nature
a temperate climate preceding storm.)

3

Snow déjà vu.
Every snowflake a thumbprint,
freeze-framed; dendrite crystals and arctic-
anæsthetized nerves.

—

Circling and circling and always arrive at the same
lack of conclusion:
What the cold feels like is ...
What the cold feels like is ...
What the cold feels like ...

O spit-on-it spit-on-it ... The cold

is always a predictable shock (a doomed man waiting for the blade to drop).
Ice-gleaming metal. Sting and
so cold you barely feel your tongue-tip your tongue
rip out of your mouth
or your limbs *Where are my legs? I can't feel my arms.*

... winter-dark and *Where's the bloody socket?*

4

Everything fades to . . .

Whiteout. Hypnotic and nose-close to hypothermia.
Blizzard-blinding (snow like something out of *Fargo*).
Winter a mile-high silver screen

tarnished to monotone. Unrelenting;
an eight-months' sustained
sub-zero note.

—

Look down,
look down,
look waaay down . . .

It's as if you were never here (you start to believe this).
Walk the same footprints every day
and every day they disappear — drowning
in the whiteness of it all, hyper-invisibly visible;
white trudging white.

5

Snow paranoia.

*Run! Run! The sky's falling! The sky's falling! The sky's
losing all sense of itself . . .*

phut phut phut. Feet futility on snow.
Limbs falling everywhere (flailing arms and legs
running on the spot . . .).

Night palsy. Nightmares ice-
incapacitated: disembodied snow prints, decapitated
snow angels.

—

Weather apparitions.
Glacial ghosts? Snow golems?
(Unsullied snow sticky enough to fashion limbs from.)

6

You know this climate like the shape of your hand inside your mitt;
increasing numbness (face licked with cold, ice-slick
questions on your tongue, answers
fewer than you have fingers to count on), familiarity

an avalanche
waiting . . .

Erín Moure

Little Theatres

"Poetry is doing nothing but using losing and refusing and pleasing and betraying and caressing nouns," said Gertrude Stein. Each of these new poems of Erín Moure's is a "little theatre" of the noun, seizing it in the fact of its quotidian, and meeting it as fresh, necessary, and incredulous utterance. If we say "water," she shows in her limpid cadence, we must reinvent it, not excluding oil spills, endangered aquatic birds, millwheels, and all the other economies that inflect perception. Here, poetry is urgently and simply our water, the other language that brings us, with Moure's characteristically rigorous sensuality, a thinking adequate to the damages, and the delights, of the world. Among her inventions is the heteronym Elisa Sampedrín, a pseudonymous personality whose theoretical reflections on theatre interrupt and decorate the lucidity of Moure's lyric, showing all voice to be part masque. This book includes a useful dictionary that shows other words for electrical monopoly, spontaneous whoops in song, and thanking.

from ATURUXOS CALADOS

Shirred up, wet against the grain

silica might call out

                    its finger to the chest

pressed me still :

That day we passed between the two Toledos

anos annals années a-néantes espidas pido pidas

: rain's hoof-marks

Horses shirred sleeping in wet fields

Regard a tree.

Who would have better seized light's longing?

Longing a labour is first, is first.

First the cold path of it. (Bring water.) Egregious

        is a few steps over wet stones

        ai ailala

        or you might miss it

That limitless strophe

        : month

Sage   or wary

Physically   song's capacity

obriga cargada

    onérous

    these days.

na hortiña do espello (¿espello?)

espiñas

as espiñas dos borrachos do neón

os borrachos do comprensible, do entendemento

estendido

ningures

o son   aire   rumor

en consecuencia

moi poucas palabriñas

cortesías

menos as poldras do pensamento,

empurradas do lonxe.

para María do Cebreiro

Did I have seized ruckus

Job's weir

      catching (outcome) these fishes

      and old leaves

me in the mill house at La Chaux

it all broken down, stone pushed into

auga agua eaux

Writing's 'succumb' with great

              happiness.

from EIGHT LITTLE THEATRES OF THE CORNICES
by Elisa Sampedrín

THEATRE OF THE GREEN LEIRA (MANDÚA)

Is bad weather coming
how would we know
Is bad weather coming
call everyone

I am all alone cutting the grass or grain
cutting the wood I am alone
splitting it open carrying it to the crib
Call everyone, put the white table out in the yard
sharpen the knives the scythes
bring out the books now
sharpen the clock's knives too

where did we read any of this
my heart mad with beating
I might lie down here in this field before you come

call everyone
the flies are singing their hymnal hum hum ai ai
how would we know

the needles of the clock are cutting down the names of the hours

THEATRE OF THE STONE CHAPEL (ABADES)

In one of its cornices are the two boots of a man
In one of the stone canzorros
If you listen you can hear him walk
His walk is stone and
his gasoline is stone
and his quill is stone

that's why he hasn't written
because his quill is stone

that's why he hasn't come yet
his gasoline is stone

that's why at night you hear him walking
his boots are stone

even his field of corn is stone
and his mother is water

THEATRE OF THE HOPE OF A CEBOLA (SANTISO)

On the hill there is no hay
but rain

no hay for a hayrick but
small rivulets singing the grass down

An onion has toppled off a high cart
the chest of the high cart has gone on past the hill

if pressed with a shoe an onion toppled
may take root

Will a shoe ever find it
how can we know

will the onion find a mouth to eat it
how can we ever know

In the channels of water :
small blue rivulets of blue

THEATRE OF THE MILLO SECO (BOTOS)

I am in the little field of my mother
Her field touches
oaks of the valley
and I touch the faces of my corn

Opening corn's faces
so that my hands touch its braille letters
The face of corn is all in braille
the corn wrote it

Fires will burn this evening
burn the dry husks of the corn
and I will learn to read
Sheep will wait by the trough
for they know corn's feature, corn's humility

corn's dichten

grain's

granite too

from ELISA SAMPEDRÍN, SOME BITS ON LITTLE THEATRES

In little theatres the search for form is abandoned. This is its form.

*

Little theatres does not mess with the "dramatic fact of a mystery." It does not try to finish the audience's sentences.

*

Some have said little theatres is minimalist. But this is not strictly so. Whatever else is stripped away in minimalism, and so much, I guess, is indeed "stripped away," a rhetorical convention remains. But rhetoric takes time, and it is time that has been stripped away from little theatres, as it has been from life.

*

Critics have said little theatres is unsatisfactory, primarily this, unsatisfactory. But this is like saying the alphabet is unsatisfactory. Do you expect the alphabet to come up with words for you?

XIIV   ORA E LABORA

The intent was to never sleep with knives
but to be clothed and belted
bieitiniñas ready to sing out every hour
so one life's oration can save 10M

In case of new bombardments we need more like us
saving lives by refusing to sleep with knives

Well maybe a bit more, maybe corn cutting too

Wind plays the chimneys of Galiza a faint guitar
Would it make you scared slightly too at night
It means rain's coming, auga trying to decipher clouds

In my latin, words have gone missing for centuries now
In my latin, whole letters of the alphabet
can't be read today

In your language can you say mencer ao mencer
Does that mean
dawn at dawn

ah ah
good

premonition works in your language too

Kamau Brathwaite is an internationally celebrated poet, performer, and cultural theorist. Born in Barbados, he was educated at Cambridge and the University of Sussex. He co-founded the Caribbean Artists Movement and is a long-serving cultural advisor to the Government of Barbados. Brathwaite has authored many works, including *The Zea Mexican Diary, Middle Passages, Ancestors,* and *The Development of Creole Society, 1770–1820.* His numerous honours include the Neustadt International Prize for Literature, the Bussa Award, the Casa de las Américas Prize, the Charity Randall Prize for Performance and Written Poetry, and Guggenheim and Fulbright fellowships. He has taught at the University of the West Indies, Southern Illinois University, the University of Nairobi, Boston University, Holy Cross College, and Yale and was a visiting fellow at Harvard. Brathwaite is currently a professor of comparative literature at New York University.

Durs Grünbein is the author of eight previous volumes of poetry as well as several essay collections and translations from the Greek and Latin. His work has been awarded many major German literary prizes, including the highest, the Georg-Büchner-Preis, which he won at age thirty-three, and the Friedrich-Nietzsche-Preis. Grünbein's collections of poetry include *Grauzone morgens, Schädelbasislektion, Falten und Fallen,* and *Nach den Satiren.* In 1995, he received the Peter Huchel Prize for Poetry. Among the plays from antiquity of which he has written new translations are Aeschylus' *The Persians* and Seneca's *Thyestes.* Grünbein's work, which also includes contributions to catalogues and a libretto for opera, has been translated into many languages. He has lived in Berlin since 1985.

Phil Hall grew up in rural Ontario. His first book, *Eighteen Poems,* was published in Mexico City in 1973. Since then he has published eight other books of poems, three chapbooks, and a cassette of labour songs. His books of poetry include *Why I Haven't Written* and *The Unsaid.* In 2001, his collection *Trouble Sleeping* was nominated for the Governor General's Literary Award for Poetry. The title of *An Oak Hunch* is the author's homage to a poetic mentor, Al Purdy. Hall, who holds an M.A. in creative writing from the University of Windsor, has taught writing and literature at York University, Ryerson University, the Kootenay School of Writing, and a number of colleges. He has been the literary editor of *This* magazine and is editor and publisher of Flat Singles Press. He teaches poetry at George Brown College and Canadian literature at Seneca College, both in Toronto.

Michael Hofmann was born in West Germany and grew up in England. He did his postgraduate studies at the University of Regensburg and Trinity College, Cambridge. He has worked as a freelance writer, translator, and reviewer. The son of the German novelist Gert Hofmann, his translation of his father's novel *The Film Explainer* won *The Independent*'s Foreign Fiction Prize. He has also translated work by Bertolt Brecht, Joseph Roth, Herta Mueller, and Franz Kafka. Hofmann has twice won the Schlegel-Tieck Prize, for his adaptation of *The Double Bass* by Patrick Süskind and his translation of Wolfgang Koeppen's *Death in Rome*. Hofmann's published poetry includes *Nights in the Iron Hotel*, which won the Cholmondeley Award, and *Acrimony*, which won the Geoffrey Faber Memorial Prize. He co-edited *After Ovid: New Metamorphoses* with James Lasdun. *Behind the Lines*, a collection of Hofmann's reviews, was published in 2001. He lives in London.

Sylvia Legris is originally from Winnipeg, Canada. *Nerve Squall* is her third book-length collection of poetry and is also shortlisted for the Pat Lowther Memorial Award. Her poems have been published in many journals, including *Border Crossings, Room of One's Own*, and *CV2*. Her previous books are *iridium seeds* and *circuitry of veins*. Legris has twice been nominated for a Pushcart Prize, Best of the Small Presses Series, and in 2001 won the *Malahat Review*'s Long Poem Prize for "Fishblood Sky." Legris also received an honourable mention in the poetry category of the 2004 National Magazine Awards. She lives in Saskatoon, Canada.

Dunya Mikhail was born in Iraq and worked as Literary Editor for *The Baghdad Observer*. Facing increasing threats and harassment from the Iraqi authorities for her writings, she fled Iraq in the late 1990s and studied Near Eastern Studies at Wayne State University. In 2001, she was awarded the U.N. Human Rights Award for Freedom of Writing. Mikhail has published four collections of poetry in Arabic (she speaks and writes in Arabic, Aramaic, and English) and one lyrical, multi-genre text, *The Diary of a Wave Outside the Sea*. She currently lives in Michigan.

Erín Moure is a poet and translator based in Montreal with twelve books of poetry to her credit. Her 2002 collection, *O Cidadán*, was a finalist for the Governor General's Literary Award. *Sheep's Vigil by a Fervent Person*, her translation from the Portuguese of Alberto Caeiro/Fernando Pessoa's *O Guardador de Rebanhos*, was a finalist for the Griffin Poetry Prize and the City of Toronto Book Award. Both *The Frame of a Book/A Frame of the Book* and *Pillage Laud* appeared in 1999. *Search Procedures* was a finalist for the Governor General's Literary Award, *Furious* was awarded the Governor General's Literary Award for Poetry, and *WSW* received a QSPELL poetry prize. *Little Theatres* won the A. M. Klein Prize for Poetry, was nominated for the Governor General's Literary Award for Poetry, and is also shortlisted for the Pat Lowther Memorial Award. Moure is currently writer-in-residence at the University of New Brunswick.

Michael Palmer was born in New York City. He is the author of numerous books of poetry, including *Blake's Newton, The Circular Gates, Without Music, Notes for Echo Lake, First Figure, Sun, At Passages, The Lion Bridge: Selected Poems 1972–1995, The Promises of Glass*, and *Codes Appearing: Poems 1979–1988*. Palmer's work has appeared in literary magazines such as *Boundary 2, Berkeley Poetry Review, Sulfur, Conjunctions*, and *O-blek*. His honours include two grants from the Literature Program of the National Endowment for the Arts and a Guggenheim Foundation fellowship. In 1999, Palmer was elected a Chancellor of the Academy of American Poets. He lives in San Francisco.

Elizabeth Winslow is a fiction writer and a graduate of the Iowa Writers' Workshop. Her translation of Dunya Mikhail's *The War Works Hard* won the PEN prize for translation in 2004 and was published in 2005 in the U.S.A. by New Directions (and simultaneously in Canada by Penguin). She has had other translated poems published in *Modern Poetry in Translation, Poetry International, Words Without Borders, Circumference*, and *World Literature Today*, as well as short stories and nonfiction published in *Phoebe, Blue Mesa Review, Louisville Review*, and *Variety*.

ACKNOWLEDGEMENTS

The publisher thanks the following for their kind permission to reprint the work contained in this volume:

The excerpt from "Hawk" from *Born to Slow Horses* by Kamau Brathwaite is reprinted by permission of Wesleyan University Press.

"Portrait of the Artist as a Young Border Dog (Not Collie)" from *Ashes for Breakfast* by Durs Grünbein (translated by Michael Hofmann) is reprinted by permission of Farrar, Straus and Giroux.

"Homage," "The," "So," "A," "As," "Crease," "This," "But," "Soon," and "Dream of a Language That Speaks" from *Company of Moths* by Michael Palmer are reprinted by permission of New Directions Books.

"America," "The Resonance," "The Theory of Absence," "Nothing Here Is Enough," and "What's New?" from *The War Works Hard* by Dunya Mikhail (translated by Elizabeth Winslow) are reprinted by permission of New Directions Books.

The excerpt from "Gank Pluck" and "Index of First Lines" from *An Oak Hunch* by Phil Hall are reprinted by permission of Brick Books.

"Strange Birds; Twitching Birds" and "Agitated Sky Etiology" from *Nerve Squall* by Sylvia Legris are reprinted by permission of Coach House Books.